The Spirit Of New Orleans

McKnight Family Chronicles of Hurricane Katrina

Sandra McKnight

ISBN 978-0-615-32705-1

Published By
DeLaSandra McKnight
www.ladymcknight.com

Wikipedia contributors, "Timeline of Hurricane Katrina," *Wikipedia, The Free Encyclopedia,* http://en.wikipedia.org/w/index.php?title=Timeline_of_Hurricane_Katrina&oldid=308217251 (accessed August 16, 2008)

Acknowledgments

Thank You to my dear husband Rodney McKnight, my children and step children, Lanette Pruitt aka 'Auntie Red', the Roberts family, Mayor Ray Nagin, the City of Houston and Mayor Bill White.

&

Thank you to Bishop Darryl S. Brister (for laying before God and lighting my path), my favorite cousin/sister Hassann Curry, Althea Edwards, Kristi Corse, Karen Chambers, Mary Spain (for your editing assistance), Jeff Taebel & H-GAC.

Contents

A Poetic Tribute

August 29, 2005, the day God shook the nation, with the destruction of one of His valued creations by the winds and rains of the Katrina Devastation.

The day a soul died, a spirit fled, a distinct culture was captured…then led astray.

> *New Orleans, My Home,*
> *The Essence of Me*

It was February 18, 1969, Mardi Gras Day, when a southern belle with child awoke to prepare for her day of celebration… ready to shout!
" Laissez les bon temps rouler! (lay-zay lay bon ton rule-ay)"

> *Our Creole Cry for "Let the Good Times Roll!"*

Feeling a bit ill she decided to take an ole' time remedy called three 6's cold medicine, and instead of heading to the Zulu parade, she was headed straight for Charity Hospital to give birth to her first precious baby girl, two months early.

Yes ya'll, that precious baby girl was me! Born on a day that this Mystic Society presented parades, ball masks, parties and celebration for the enjoyment of its residents and invited guests.

New Orleans may have been a small city in which a person could literally walk from one end and cross the city line in a matter of hours - not much land to miss - but inside that bowl held whole lot'a rhythm, a whole lot'a flavor, and a whole lot'a tradition that was distinctive, unique and irreplaceable in comparison to any other city in the nation.

I think about playing outside just after the rain, when the streets were flooded sometimes up to my knees. We had some fun in that water, ya'll!

I think about my peaceful rides on the street car looking at the big mansion homes through the Garden District, imagining what they might look like on the inside, and even getting a sneak peak into a few on my way to work each morning.

I remember the creamy taste of praline candy, sweet huck-a-bucks and drive thru Daiquiri Shops.

I think about sneaking away to Café Du monde at 2 o'clock in the morning to sit in the outside café' and enjoy my chicory coffee and beignets, while watching the couples walk along the river view every now and again.

Being the city that never sleeps, there were always great things to do in the Big Easy.

Like Sunday's on the Lake Front with Shrimp Po-Boys and Crawfish boils,

Like the Reggae Nights and the Black Heritage Festivals, the second lines to celebrate the Funerals, Weddings, New Births or damn near anything for that matter.

Like late evening poetry readings with live Jazz bands emphasizing every hook.

Like riding the steam boat just to get to the zoo which was always free to mothers on Mother's Day.
Like spending a romantic evening, circling the streets in the horse and carriage.

I will definitely miss New Orleans.

Even if the city is revived, the tradition and lagniappe (the little extra) will be gone.

The down home southern hospitality, that says "you'd betta not come to my house and don't eat nothin'!"

And because of its Catholic undertone most of the city ate only fish on Fridays during Lent.

Whether they were Catholic or not!

New Orleaneans had a way of doing things our own way. We had a way of living like everybody was family, laughing and enjoying each other every day.

We had a true freedom that before now I didn't realize existed.

New Orleans was not just a city, but an essence that invoked its spirit into the people who lived there.

It became the Jazz in our walk, and the way we talk and express our points of view.

It became the buck jump in our praise, our love for life and joy of living each day.

As long as I live I will never forget that vibe, because forgetting the Spirit of New Orleans, is like forgetting me.

Chapter 1

Leaving Home

Saturday, August 27, 2005

Goodness that phone is going to wake the baby, I thought as I tried to quickly catch it before the next ring.

"Mom?" It was Sharice, my 17 year old daughter bellowing through the receiver, from her part-time job at Curves. She sounded frightened. "What's wrong Reeci?" "Did you hear about the storm that's coming? It's all over the news and they're saying we need to evacuate! We're listening to it right now at work! What are we gonna do?" "What storm? I asked, "No, I haven't heard anything". I rarely watched the news. *I've since learned that lesson.* "It's on all the stations, turn on the TV!" "Alright, Sharice, I'll check it out and let you know."

I hung up the phone and walked into the living room where my newly appointed Associate Pastor husband was getting ready to take the Soldiers of Light out to evangelize. He looked so handsome in his military fatigues.

"Sharice just called talking about a big storm that's supposed to be coming and that we need to evacuate", I informed him.

I turned on the TV in the living room. Mayor Ray Nagin was on air. He looked very depressed. I don't remember everything he said but I do remember him saying "I've got a bad feelin' about this one, ya'll". You could feel the weight of his seriousness through the big screen television. "I've already put my family on the plane out of here, but I have to stay behind and go down with the ship.

There's a major storm heading our way and it doesn't look good for us at all. They won't let me declare a mandatory evacuation yet, but I will declare one tomorrow if this thing is still on the same course, whether they let me or not." He talked about wanting to get buses and trains to board the people on but the governor wouldn't let him do it.

I looked at my husband and he looked at me and said "ya'll pack up, we're heading out at midnight.

One thing I'd learned was to trust my husband's judgment in matters like this. I was nonchalant to say the least, due to our previous evacuation mishaps.

We were instructed to evacuate last year while I was on mandatory bed rest and risked the birth of my son. We sat in traffic *16 hours* traveling to Houston, which was normally a five hour trip and the storm turned and missed us. Then earlier this year they said we had to evacuate, but to my relief, my husband said no we'll stay, and we didn't get a drop of rain.

Somewhere in my spirit, I thought that New Orleans would never receive the devastation that Florida did due to the amount of praying the people in our city did. Hurricane George in '96, was my first experience of hearing people pray on the radio.

Here were more God-fearing, praying people than I'd ever known in my life; therefore I knew that God wouldn't let anything happen to us or our city, even if, Bourbon street was like Sodom and Gomorrah.

After the last storm missed us I proclaimed these beliefs out loud, and God responded through the mouth of Bishop Brister, our church Pastor. "Don't believe that we're exempt! Just because it didn't hit us this time doesn't mean it won't. Some of you are saying, yeah, New Orleans is too blessed to be hit the way Florida was" (which was my exact words), "but we aren't", he said "there could always be a next time."

My exact words often fell from the lips of this man of God, which was my reason for staying under his anointed teaching since the first time I'd heard him speak.

I remembered feeling convicted and knew God was talking to me. I started packing everything the baby owned.

Tell me if this isn't God...
About three weeks earlier, Christina (my best friend) called and posed a hypothetical question. She said "if something was to happen, you had to leave in a hurry, and never come back and could only take three things what would they be?" I gave her four, "my family, each person's personal file folder, my CPU and my pictures". This conversation rang in my head as I packed our things. We didn't have space for the CPU with it's hard drive but now I carry a flash drive in my purse.

I spent that afternoon at the lake front with my son, a favorite spot for the residents of New Orleans on Sundays. The park was large and spanned for miles around the lake.

The lake was so large that there is no other side, at least as far as the eye could see.

People would do all sorts of things while they enjoyed time with their families and friends. Many would be fishing, or sitting on the benches near the water or on the steps of the levee. Others would be in the park, eating shrimp or enjoying crawfish boils or barbeques.

The kids would be on one of the various play grounds or rolling down the side of the great hill of grass that separated the park from the lake front homes.

Some people walked the top of the hill for exercise, while others played ball in the plains below. You would hear the thunderous roar of the motorcycles as they would whiz through, trying to stunt (show off).

There were birthday parties, study groups and all sorts of activities going on at the lake front on Sundays.
The main thing we did was relax and enjoy time with our friends and family. New Orleans has two of these parks, where the water that surrounded the city met land on each side. One was the lake front and on the other side of town was the river view, which was near my house. Both were packed on Sundays.

I spent the afternoon trying to get my 11-month-old little man-boy to walk. He would stand, but he wouldn't step, unless I put him the walker, then he'd have the nerve to try and run. We spent hours playing and lying on our blanket, watching people enjoy the day. This did not look like the weekend for a storm, especially not the hurricane Mayor Nagin spoke about. It was a truly beautiful day.

The only family member who was staying behind that I was concerned about was my Aunt Red, "Auntie", my mother's youngest sister. Most of my family who still lived in New Orleans, were pretty much self sufficient, but Auntie Red lived alone about 20 minutes away, in Waveland, Ms. which is right outside of Biloxi.

I called to see if she wanted to evacuate with us. "No, baby, I'm not going anywhere" she said. I can't leave Ms. Margaret." Ms. Margaret was the elderly lady who lived next door to my aunt.

Most of Auntie's working career was spent taking care of the elderly in convalescent homes and hospice care facilities, so after my aunt could no longer work, she would sit with the elderly in her neighborhood to keep them company, cook, clean, run errands or do whatever they needed. She had become particularly close to her next door neighbor, Ms. Margaret. My aunt knew that Ms. Margaret's family lived out of state and that the elderly woman would be alone.

"Me and Ms. Margaret will be just fine in here, baby, don't you worry about us, ya'll go 'head. I'll see you when you get back." Auntie was pretty stubborn. When she had her mind fixed to do something, nothing could change her mind.

Honestly, none of us were really worried. We all thought the most we would get is a little rain. I basked in the thoughts that this would be a weekend visit to Houston and we'd be home by Wednesday at the latest. For myself, I only packed flip-flops, sweat pants, T-shirts (for five days) and one dress and pumps for church on Sunday. I expected a nice vacation where my in-laws would be doting so much over the baby that I would have some relaxation and "me" time.

My husband, four of our children, our granddaughter and I headed out about 1^{AM} and made it to Houston around 7^{AM}. Smooth sailing all the way. "Glory to God"! We slept most of that day.

By that evening, the rest of my in-laws who were evacuating from New Orleans, were there. By the end of the day, we had 23 people in that large three bedroom house. We set up the barbeque pits, ate and watched the news that entire day.

My father-in-law, brother- in law and his wife, decided to stay home and stick it out. They lived a few miles from each other so they figured they would be alright if they needed anything, until it was over.
But according to the news, there was much need for concern...

"Just after midnight, at 12:40^{AM}, Hurricane Katrina reached Category 4 intensity with 145 mph winds." The newscaster intensly informed the broadcasting audience. "By 7^{AM}, it was a Category 5 storm, with maximum sustained winds of 175 mph.

In a press conference at roughly 10^{AM}, Mayor C. Ray Nagin declared that "a mandatory evacuation order is hereby called for all of the Parish of Orleans." "We're facing the storm most of us have feared," he told the early-morning news conference, with the governor at his side. Following Nagin's speech, Governor Blanco stated that President Bush called her "just before" the press conference and said that he was "concerned about the storm's impact" and asked her "to please ensure that there would be a mandatory evacuation of New Orleans." Katrina was expected to make landfall overnight. Shortly after the meeting, the National Weather Service issued a bulletin predicting "devastating" damage.

At 12^{PM}, the Louisiana Superdome was opened as a "refuge of last resort" for those residents that were unable to obtain safe transport out of the city.

President Bush declared a state of emergency in Alabama and Mississippi, and a major disaster in Florida.

We couldn't believe what we were hearing. All of the adults were huddled around the TV or radio stations, tuning into the hurricane broadcasts or making calls trying to reach their loved ones to see who was still in the city and who had made it out.

Monday, August 29, 2005

At 6:10^{AM}, Hurricane Katrina made its second landfall as a strong Category 3 hurricane near Buras-Triumph, Louisiana, with sustained winds of more than 125 mph, although Category 4 winds may have briefly affected the area. Katrina also made landfall in St. Bernard parish and St. Tammany parish as a Category 3 hurricane for a total of three landfalls in Louisiana.

By 8^{AM}, in New Orleans, water was seen rising on both sides of the Industrial Canal.

Everybody at the house in Houston was on edge. We knew that New Orleans was like a big bowl, six feet below sea level, and if the water reached over the levee the whole city would be under water. Even though I knew this and had heard my mother proclaim this most of my life, I still couldn't imagine that it really meant the city would be under water. No way.

At approximately 8:14^AM, the New Orleans office of the National Weather Service issued a Flash Flood Warning for Orleans Parish and St Bernard Parish, citing a levee breach at the Industrial Canal. The National Weather Service predicted three to eight feet of water and advised people in the warning area to "move to higher ground immediately."

By 9^AM, there was six to eight feet of water in the Lower Ninth Ward.

At 10^AM, while at a Medicare event in El Mirage, Arizona, President Bush said, "I want to thank the governors of the affected regions for mobilizing assets prior to the arrival of the storm to help citizens avoid this devastating storm."

Also, at 10^AM, Hurricane Katrina made its third landfall near Pearlington, Mississippi and Slidell, Louisiana, with sustained winds of 120 mph after crossing Breton Sound.

"Oh My God! That's right near Auntie Red!" I grabbed my cell, and was still unable to get through.

Chapter 2

The Power of Prayer

Auntie went next door to Ms. Margaret's house about 8^AM. The sky was dark and the thunder was louder than she'd ever heard before. She heard a loud boom and a rumble and could feel the ground shake underneath the house. She went to the window to see what she could.

Suddenly, a big wave of water came rushing through the parking lot. It came out of nowhere and burst the front door open!

Auntie ran to the door and pushed with all her strength to close the door. She fell against the wall and tried to push the door closed with her foot but the water was too strong and too fast.

Auntie got a glimpse of Ms. Margaret as her elderly neighbor slipped underneath the water. She scurried through the water that had reached her chest by this time and grabbed hold of Ms. Margaret to lift her head out of the water that tried to capture her fate.

Auntie considered climbing out of the window and on top the roof, but Ms. Margaret was 82 years old and my aunt knew the old lady wouldn't make it.

Instead, she picked up her elderly neighbor and tried to hang her arms over the curtain rod, but it broke because of the weight and they slipped underneath the water again.

Auntie had a firm grip on Ms. Margaret and refused to let her go. She again picked up her neighbor and in her panic managed to balance the elderly woman on top the ceiling fan.

Neither of the women could swim, so they needed to move quickly before this water rose above their heads. Auntie managed to get herself over to a door. She stepped one foot up on top of the door knob, stood her other foot on the door knob on the other side and held her hands on to the top of that door for dear life as the water continued to rise.

"Ms. Margaret, it's gonna be alright" my Aunt tried to assure her hysterical neighbor, "Lord God please make it alright!"

"Let's Pray Ms. Margaret, Let's Pray! My Aunt shouted over the water that had now settled right at their mouths. The women had enough space to breathe when they held their heads back. And they prayed.

The women remained in that filthy water, crying and calling out to God for several hours.   Ms. Margaret repented for her sins as she cried and called for help.

Auntie was praying "PLEASE GOD SAVE US, make this water go down! If you make this water go down Lord, I promise I'll read your word day and night! Please Lord God make this water go down!" she cried.

Then she prayed for forgiveness. "Father God Please Forgive Me, if I can't save Ms. Margaret." She was afraid that there may come a moment when she had no more strength and couldn't keep Ms. Margaret's head up over this water, and that death would come upon her. She was deeply afraid for Ms. Margaret, so my Aunt continued to earnestly pray. As those women prayed the water started to go down.

Once they were freed from the captivity of the water, Auntie sat Ms. Margaret in a safe spot and walked to search for help. She was about a mile or so down the road, when Ms. Margaret's son and his family's car turned the bend.

They picked up my Aunt and headed back to the house. Ms. Margaret was elated to see her family and she cried. Auntie walked across the drive way to her own house and experienced more devastation as she saw her own home destroyed. Thankful that God had spared her life, she picked up her soggy purse and turned to leave. She was greeted at the door by an alligator!

Chapter 3

Lost

We all had been trying to contact everyone we knew all morning, who were possibly still in the New Orleans area but their phones were out of order, and all we were getting was that stupid message from the cell provider.

We needed to know about Auntie Red, My father-in-law (Mr. Mac) and Bobby and Lynell (my brother-in-law and his wife).

The whole house in Houston was in horror as we watched scenes of New Orleans on the morning news.

By 11^{AM}, there was approximately 10 feet of water in St. Bernard Parish. Many rooftops could not be seen here as they were submerged. Therefore, there was much more than 10 feet of water in many places.

At 2 PM, New Orleans officials confirmed a breach of the 17th Street Canal levee. There was also confirmation of breaches at two other canals.

In a press conference at 3 PM, New Orleans Homeland Security Director Terry Ebbertt stated that he was positive that there were casualties resulting from the storm, based on calls to emergency workers from people trapped in trees and homes. He said that, "Everybody who had a way or wanted to get out of the way of this storm was able to. For some that didn't, it was their last night on this earth." Police were fanning out across the city to assess damage, rescue people, and get a good look at the situation before nightfall. The hardest-hit areas of the city were the Lower

Ninth Ward, New Orleans East, Gentilly, Lakeview, St. Bernard parish, and Plaquemines parish.

My home!!! My home was gone!!! Right there on the television in front of me...Our people were dying!!!

There was crying and panic in the house that day.

According to the news...Governor Blanco ordered 68 school buses into New Orleans from surrounding parishes to begin evacuating any survivors that remained in the city.

FEMA Director Michael Brown also urged local fire and rescue departments outside Louisiana, Alabama, and Mississippi not to send trucks or emergency workers into disaster areas without an explicit request for help from state or local governments.

Brown sought the approval from Homeland Security Secretary Michael Chertoff five hours after landfall to dispatch 1,000 Homeland Security workers into the region.

Brown acknowledged that this process would take two days. He described Katrina as a "near catastrophic event."

Brown defined the role of requested assigned personnel and additional aid from the United States Department of Homeland Security: "Establish and maintain positive working relationships with disaster affected communities and the citizens of those communities. Collect and disseminate information and make referrals for appropriate assistance. Identification of potential issues within the community and reporting to appropriate personnel. Convey a positive image of disaster operations to government officials, community organizations and the general public. Perform outreach with community leaders on available Federal disaster assistance."

President Bush declared a major disaster for Louisiana, Mississippi, and Alabama.

Chapter 4

Your Will Be Done

"Heeeeelp!" Auntie screamed as she searched for a way to escape the alligator that was moving toward her. Pop! Pop!

Mr. Leroy, one of Auntie's neighbor's from around the corner came by to check on my aunt, and heard her screams for help. "I'm glad I brought my gun", he said as he picked up the dead alligator and slung it out of the door behind him.

Praise God! My Aunt yelled as she rushed over to her life saver. Mr. Leroy had shot that alligator dead. He and Auntie slushed through the water and out of the house.

Tuesday, August 30, 2005

At 12^{PM}, Homeland Security became aware that the New Orleans levee breaches could not be plugged. Governor Blanco ordered that all of New Orleans, including the Superdome, be evacuated due to the flooding of the city.

She commandeered hundreds of buses from across Louisiana, and those buses eventually evacuated more than 15,000 people who were stranded in the city by Thursday, September 1st. There were also many instances reported of looting, including looting by police officers. Governor Blanco also said that she would request President Bush send federal troops to help restore law and order in New Orleans.

We still hadn't heard anything from Mr. Mac, Bobby or Auntie. I began to get antsy and called the police in Houston to ask if they could get a message into the National Guard or the police in New Orleans and Waveland to let them know that our family's were in their homes and would need to be rescued. I gave them their addresses and prayed that God would keep His mighty hand of protection upon them as they endured.

Most people would call this lady absolutely crazy, but do you know after all that horror, my Aunt decided she *didn't* want to be rescued by Ms. Margaret's son. He asked her if they could take her somewhere, but she had no idea where she would go. All of the family was gone. Besides that she couldn't stop thinking about Ms. Vera, another elderly lady, who lived around the corner. She'd spoken with her earlier that morning and knew that the lady would be home alone. The car was full anyway, and there wouldn't be enough room for the both of them, so she declined rescue.

Personally, I would have found a spot in that car even if I had to ride in the trunk! And I wouldn't care where they were going, just get me the heck out of here!
But not Auntie, she needed to go check on her neighbor. Auntie Red herself was in her mid 50's and to me she was definitely out of her mind, but she was only being Auntie.

This was the same kind of spirit most of the women on my mother's side of my family carried. Their concern was always for another, so much so that they would give their last drop of life for the benefit of another-truly good-hearted women, with a heart after God's own heart. I pray that I could be half the woman they were and live up to their spiritual legacy.

Auntie and Mr. Leroy found Ms. Vera sitting in the parking lot of the Dollar General store with a group of people who had survived the storm.   Ms. Vera was able to get into the attic of her house and find safety there until the water went down.

They waited for rescue in the Dollar General parking lot until dark but no one came, so the two women walked back to Ms. Vera's house.

They pulled the leather couch outside and underneath the carport. Thank God it was a couch bed. They opened it up and took the wet mattress off and slept on the spring.

Wednesday, August 31, 2005

Hurricane Katrina is finally downgraded to a tropical depression. Mayor Ray Nagin announced that the planned sandbagging of the 17th Street Canal levee breach had failed. At the time, 85% of the city was underwater.

In Houston, we watched as the news helicopters showed us our people stranded on roof tops, begging for help. We watched to see if we recognized any of the bodies floating in the water.

This was the most horrific experience of our lives, waiting to hear word if our family members and friends were dead or alive.

But being that this was New Orleans, a place where everybody was family, the pain and fear was there for the entire population that was left behind.

My husband's sisters were crying for fear of what had become of their father and brother. This family was extremely close. My husband lived alone with his dad most of his life after the divorce, yet he stayed strong and didn't shed a tear for the encouragement of his sisters.

I was so busy crying and being terrified about what could be happening to my Aunt that I forgot that he may have needed to cry too. Instead my husband, my man of God, covered me.

Day and night for four days my Aunt and Ms. Vera slept underneath that carport. The sewer smell the water left behind began to make them sick. Each day they made their way up to the dollar general to see if rescue would arrive.

Back in Houston, Wednesday night was Bible Study at my sister-in-law's church. Since Rodney was a Pastor of Beacon Light's Evangelism Ministry in New Orleans, a student of the Bible College, and a member of the church for many years, the only thing he knew to do *was* to go to church. Beacon Light helped shape him into the great man that he is today. Bishop Brister had a way of making the men of his church accountable for being good, wholesome and responsible men of God. Belonging to that ministry made them strive for excellence in their personal lives by invoking vision and establishing goals and structure.

This is where my husband and I met, serving together as "Soldiers of Light".

Every other Saturday about 30 members of our ministry would meet up in the church parking lot to go out and win souls to Christ!

At 12 noon we would begin with praise and worship. Praising God in song for all He's done in our lives.

The praise songs used to pump me up! I used to be clappin' all hard, singing all loud and off key. And after we were all praised out, we would fall into worship songs.

My husband is really good at leading us into worship. By the time we were finished we were filled with the anointing of the Holy Spirit. We would keep the momentum and the peace as we loaded into the vans. We dressed in black and white camouflage military pants and black ministry t-shirts, with white letters proclaiming us as Soldiers of Light.

Our positions were set up like the military too. Our Captain was my husband, the Pastor of the ministry. There was a co-captain, who was the second in command, two lieutenants, and four sergeants, who led the people when we divided into groups; if you weren't one of these than you were a private.

I remember the first time I went out to evangelize, this was under the leadership of Elder Joseph Lafrance Jr.; we went to the French Quarter. I was so excited! The French Quarter Festival was going on that weekend, so unlike a normal Saturday, there were many tourists who provided a bigger variety of culture among the residents.

And here we come, walking through the Quarter. About 15 people in a group on each side of the street singing praise songs.

Soooooldiers of Light....Move Satan...Soooooldiers of Light! We've come to glorify Jesus Christ! Move Satan!

Usually first timers were urged to stand back and just watch but Elder Lafrance, being aware of my excitement and eagerness to win souls, allowed me the freedom to talk to whomever I chose. I remember asking one gentleman if he'd accepted Jesus as his personal Lord and Savior. He responded "no I'm an atheist", and I informed him that God doesn't care what you are baby, he still loves you. That man just looked at me. Hopefully I planted a seed in him.

A lot of the people would stop and become curious as to who we were. If they approached us or if they accepted one of our fliers we would open up conversation, and ask them if they'd accepted Jesus as their personal Lord and Savior. "Huh?" was usually the first response. Then we'd ask, "If you were to die today, would you know beyond any doubt that you were going straight to heaven?" Either they knew and they would boldly state their belief or they had doubt.

To the ones who doubted, one of our sergeants or lieutenants would ask them, "May I help ensure your place in Heaven by leading you in the prayer of salvation?" "How would this prayer ensure that I will go to heaven?", many would ask. One of us would show them the scripture, Romans 10:9-13 that plainly says "if you confess with your mouth, 'Jesus is Lord,' and believe in your heart that God raised him from the dead, you will be saved."

Most people would decide that they wanted prayer, for one reason or another. We'd pray for them and their families, then ask, "now repeat this prayer after me and everyone here will be in agreement".

"Father God, In the name of Jesus, we come asking that you forgive me of my sins, come into my heart, create in me a clean heart and renew a right spirit within me. I will serve you the rest of my days. I claim the victory and I know that no weapon formed against me shall prosper because I am saved, I am saved, I am saved".

Then we would make them understand that it was not about living the perfect life, because we were all born in iniquity, but about striving to be the best we can be. And when we fall into sin, because we will fall into sin, to call on Jesus to pick us up, dust us off, and set us back on our path of purpose and excellence. This is God's guarantee for our spot in Heaven.

We'd instruct them to find a good Bible based church and learn more about their Lord and Savior. That's it, no lengthy conversation, we were on a mission! We had souls to save! "Soooodiers of Light......Move Satan!..."

We would leave them with a piece of paper that had the scripture printed on it, to remind them of the step toward Christ they made on this day and we would write down their names and pass it on to our church intercessors who continued to pray for them and their families.

I absolutely loved the ease in getting saved and living with God. For so many years, I was that girl who literally crossed the street when the witnesses would come my way. Or hide and play gone, when they'd come to the door. I cringed at the word evangelist, thinking of their persistence.

Our church was determined to bring simple understanding (plant the seed) and let God do the watering. I respected the space the ministry gave you to grow, no matter how many years it took, without judgment.

Bishop Brister always proclaimed how imperfect he was, and that he also knew, just like everyone else, God wasn't finished with him yet and he was pursuing a life of excellence. Not perfection, but to live the best that he could live in relationship with God.

Because he was a young Bishop of our generation, he spoke our language. He knew he needed to come real or not come at all to get through to us, and that he did.

Most of my life I lacked understanding in many areas. For many years I would not acknowledge Jesus. I didn't know how to. To me, this was another man and I couldn't understand who He was. I'd known all my life, deep within my spirit that there was a God, so I respected Him, but why should I acknowledge this man Jesus?

It was Bishop Darryl S. Brister of Beacon Light, who made me realize that this man "Jesus" was actually God, who'd decided to come down to earth and physically show us how to do this thing called life and get it right. God gave us principles and precepts to follow in order to live the most peaceful life that we could.

God also wanted to show us the amazing powers that we have on the inside of us and how to tap into them through our relationship with Him.

Through God's Holy Spirit, we seriously have the power to heal the sick and raise the dead. It's our Passion, Belief and Trust in God that gives us all the Power we need to do Anything.

In those six years I grew in my excitement for God, Jesus and the Holy Spirit and my husband is the same way.

At this point, all we wanted was a Word from God; Instruction from Him about what was going on and what we were to do from this moment forward.

I knew He had pushed us out of New Orleans so that He can do something new in our lives. Therefore, He had to make it right for us.

Chapter 5

A New Life

We were in Wednesday night Bible study at my sister-in-law's church, crying and praising God, all of ten minutes when in walked Bishop Brister and First Lady, our Church Pastor from New Orleans!

Bishop!!!! My husband and I almost shouted as they passed by us. We waved so hard our arms could have fallen off. Bishop was cheesin' and wavin' just as hard while he shouted his whisper to meet him after church.

We were so excited. It felt like things were coming together already. I was especially excited for my husband! This man has been the tool God used to guide my husband's for life years, and he was here, in the same church as we were, all the way in Houston, Texas.

As it turned out the Pastor of this church was friends with Bishop and had opened his home up to their family for refuge until they decided on their next move. God is amazing!!! I was sure within Bishop Brister was a "Word from the Lord".

We met with Bishop and First Lady after church, letting them know where we were and swapping stories of who we had gotten in touch with and who was left behind.

It felt so good to be in their presence and for a brief moment I could see on my husband's face relief that everything would be alright.

That night we could feel the hands of God hold us in comfort as we slept. It was the first peaceful rest we'd gotten in days. That night I had a dream...

President Bush appeared on Good Morning America, and said that he understood the frustration of Katrina victims, many of whom are still waiting for food, water, and other aid. "I fully understand people wanting things to have happened yesterday," Bush said. "I understand the anxiety of people on the ground. ... So there is frustration. But I want people to know there's a lot of help coming." He said that the government's first priority is to save lives, and described the devastation that he saw while flying over the hardest-hit areas as, "very emotional," but was also very optimistic about the prospects of New Orleans' recovery.

Daddy called! Somebody in the house shouted. The father of this family had been rescued! He, my brother-in-law and his wife were all together and had all reached safety. My father-in-law had endured tragedies during his ordeal, but he made it out alive. His story was traumatic for him and truly a sad one.

After the relief hit him, my husband finally broke down. He'd held in his fears and worry for his father and brother to remain strong for us. But after it was over, he was able to release. I felt for my baby, and I was thankful that his mom was here. I think he needed her arms, in addition to mine, in order to deeply release it all.

The family gathered around in the living room later that night. It was amazing how this three bedroom home was spacious enough to support all 23 of us comfortably.

Deciding our next moves was the topic of conversation that night.

I called FEMA and registered our family for emergency disaster assistance. Our cell phones weren't working, so there was a line for use of the home phone. As each woman finished registering her family, she would tell the intake personnel that there was another family who needed to register and she passed the phone on to the next person.

My husband and I knew that if we wanted God to move, it was time for us to move forward.

We located the addresses of the middle and high schools in the area. Then we looked up unemployment agencies, and the various assistance locations as the news stations indicated were set up for the evacuees for our refuge.

Office Team, a staffing agency, I'd worked with several years ago, sent me an e-mail, stating that if I was one of the evacuees, that I should contact their office in whatever city I was in, as soon as I was ready to go to work and they would make every effort to place me in employment with urgency. That was cool! I definitely replied to them and started that process.

Houston was truly amazing in all of the assistance they readily set up and made available for their new residents. We decided that we would get up early and make our first stop at the schools.

The main question the kids had was "When are we going home?" I couldn't help but look at them crazy. After all, these were teens we were talking to and they were watching the same news we were, but somehow, they still didn't comprehend it.

"Ok...the city is flooded," Tank, our son, interjected. "But now that the water has gone down, how many more days or weeks do you think it will take before we can go back home?" "About two years", someone said bluntly. "Honey, the city is demolished and it will take a long time before they can get it back together and rebuild the levee system good enough to let us go back". I interjected. This must have devastated their little minds, because the boys began acting out in atrocious ways at home and in school. But I won't get into that. It took a lot of patience and prayers to deal with them.

"I called my daddy, and I want to go to California", I could hear my 17-year-old daughter say, as she entered into the room during the family discussion.

My nerves began to jitter. I could feel in my spirit that this wasn't the route to take. Sharice had a 1 year old baby and being that far from me right now wouldn't be the best for her. I needed to rebuild and she needed to be with me. The last thing I needed was to worry about her and Zya. California was such a haven of bad seed, and I felt that she would get out there and would get lost.

But how do you make this decision for your 17-year-old who, just like you, feels like a burden on this family she barely knows. Two less people in this house would definitely be a relief for my sister-in-law and the other family members who complained so much about my crying grandbaby.

I began to think that this was definitely an option I needed to consider at this point, even though sirens were going off on the inside of me. This *was* after all, her senior year, I thought, trying to convince myself. Maybe it wouldn't be so bad. She is a very independent person and extremely responsible about her grades. Maybe after the year ends, we will be settled enough for her and Zya to come back home for college.

 Still, something about it didn't settle right with me. I told her that I would think about it, but this was not the best route for her. I envisioned that she would get sidetracked like so many young girls, who make the mistake of having a baby early in life.

They and their parents tend to get caught up in the idea that their error in choice has now given them a "grown-up pass" and they should be allowed to be treated as an adult. This is the area where they usually get lost.

Yes, when I found out my daughter was pregnant, my world spun out of control like every other parent in this position. After my complete and total breakdown, I began to question my relationship with God.

I shouted and cried out to God, what about all the things we had planned! We had visions and goals! What about our plans of Sharice going to a university and being successful in her goals. Hell, what about the fight it took for me to get her into this magnet school, which was about to throw her out once they find out that one of their "academically excelled" students is pregnant! I guess that fight was for nothing! What are you doing God?! Why weren't you covering her?

I walked the street car line that night for hours. I needed a word from the Lord! After I'd calmed down, I was able to hear from God.

"This changes nothing", He spoke. Then a peace came over me. I became calm and able to hear a word from the Lord. "This is her problem, not yours. Stop trying to take on all the responsibility of this error. This is not your error, this is hers. She is still a child, your child. Yes she has made a mistake, but just like any other mistake, discipline her, set additional boundaries, and move forward."

I became calm and peaceful and the Lord helped me to devise our plan. And I believed God.

I told Sharice what the Lord spoke and she was thankful that I wasn't going to kill her. She *was* grounded from dating, since she proved to be irresponsible in this area. At first, I said she would be grounded until graduation, but of course that didn't happen, but she *was* grounded for the rest of *that* year. Her curfew was earlier than normal during her pregnancy but then after the baby, I didn't have to worry about a curfew. Her responsibilities for school and for little Ms. Zya took care of that. The young man was allowed to come, visit and take care of my little granddaughter, but no dating with Sharice. Sharice had enough to deal with.

McMain Magnet School of New Orleans was very supportive to Sharice's situation. Her teachers got together and agreed that when the time came for Sharice to deliver, one of them would pick up the class work from all the other teachers and deliver them to the house. The lunch room dieticians came up with a specific diet for Sharice, with a few extra treats to help satisfy her cravings throughout the day.

Our family doctor gave her advice about how to focus on her child and education at the same time. She encouraged her with profound wisdom.

The teachers of the school and my daughter's friends got together and gave her a huge baby shower. We needed my husband's work truck to carry all the wonderful gifts home.

My mother bought the baby's crib that would turn into a toddler bed later and Sharice had just about everything the baby would need until the child would start walking.

God really worked everything out. Sharice's baby girl was born May 30th, two weeks after school ended. So she didn't have to miss school, and she had the next three months to be with her baby and to get used to motherhood before school was to start again. God delivered more bountifully than I could have ever expected and He remained true to His Word to me as I believed.

Reverse psychology was my method of getting what I knew was the "right choice" out of my head strong children. "Look, if California is where you want to be then tell your dad to send you a ticket. I have nothing stable to offer you here anyway. But I *know* that this is the wrong decision and I can feel it in my spirit! This is a set up to ruin your life! You need to stay with me."

Sharice always believed in her mother. She used to tell her friends "don't try to hide anything from my momma', she's psychic!"

While I was dealing with Sharice, the family discussion switched to the other family members. My mother-in-law and three of my sisters-in-law and their families had talked about possibly making their way to Atlanta. One of the brothers-in-law had family there. My husband, the youngest of all nine siblings, stood up and objected! "No!" He protested, we are a family and we all need to stay together! We don't need to separate!"

To me Atlanta seemed like a pretty good idea, but after seeing Bishop last night at church, I knew we were stuck in Houston. I just needed to figure out how to get us out of this house. My sister-in-law was very sweet for allowing us all to stay in her home, but Lord, she was extremely difficult for any of us to get along with, especially me, being totally unfamiliar with exactly how to deal with her. We desperately needed our own space.

"Everybody will eventually need to get on with their lives at some point", Mother Bessie, my mother-in-law interjected. Everyone had an opinion and didn't mind sharing it all at once. I tried to stay to myself and out of the way as much as possible, but unfortunately that didn't work so well.

Later on that night, Sharice came to me. "Mom you have always guided my life and if it doesn't feel right to you, then it doesn't feel right to me. If you don't want me to go to California, then I won't go".

Whew, what a relief! I think she needed to know that it was ok for her and her baby to be here in this home.

The next morning we arose early to get started with the day. Rob, my brother-in-law was in the kitchen fully dressed and pouring his coffee, when I went in. "Hey, sister-in-law, are you ready to roll?" He was about handling business and I loved that! He had energy like mine and I was ready to follow his lead. He and his wife found out where all the resource centers were, mapped them, and was ready to go.

It was amazing how we all were in the same boat but some of our people became stagnant, while others were motivated to move.

While I was one of the motivated ones, I easily became stressed and distracted by moaning and complaining. I needed to hear from God in order to get through this situation with the most ease. I needed to pray and be still within myself in order to listen to that small still voice inside that guided my moves. And most of all, I needed to have 100% confidence in the moves I made.

This was how we were taught by Bishop Brister. Faith without works is dead. Faith is an action word and you needed to move according to the guidance of the Holy Spirit on the inside of you, and your movement has to be in confidence that God is working this thing out on your behalf, regardless of what the situation looks like. I needed 100% faith surrounding me. In positivity rests the power of God on the inside of us.

But I guess this was one of my tests, to see if I would rebuke this negativity, to see if I could still find that small still voice and to see if I would move with confidence on that small, still voice. I had to muster up everything I'd learned about faith and the power that I had on the inside of me to get through this chaos.

One thing I knew for a fact, was that God had caused this to happen, therefore in this season, God *was* moving (doing a new thing in our lives), and we needed to move with God!

The next morning, we went to the school and enrolled the children. Due to the urgency of the situation, the school was accepting all New Orleans students without their documents.

The school was not used to handling this type of situation and had no definite procedures set in place, so we had to be patient as they set them up along the way. We waited patiently as the school administration figured out their new procedures for our different situations and circumstances.

 The students donated uniforms and school supplies for the children. This was both beautiful and amazing. Several hours later, the children were set up to begin their classes the next day.

From there we moved on to the unemployment office but the line was out of the door and we never made our way to the front of it before 5^{PM}. The doors closed on us.

When we got back to the house the garage door was open and there were boxes everywhere inside. The neighbors, co-workers and friends of my in-laws had dropped off boxes of toiletries, clothes and food! This was truly a blessing to us.

My mom called to inform me to start checking the mail because the nuns of her order were going to be sending us checks in the mail. There were over 200 Sisters Of St. Francis of Oldenberg who were ready to show support to me and my family. What a blessing my mom is. She always has been a sweet blessing to my life. We received about $8,000 in checks from the Sisters of St. Francis of Oldenberg community, where my mom was serving as a nun (another book).

One thing I can say, with all of us in the house, my in-laws didn't have a bill to worry about for a few months.

We still hadn't heard anything from Auntie. I began to get antsy and called the police again in Houston and asked if they could get a message to the National Guard or the police in Waveland. I asked if they could let them know that my Aunt was in her home and that we needed them to send rescue. The police officer explained that they were having trouble getting through to them due to the loss of communication towers etc., but that they were able to message in by Morse Code. He took all of the information and put it through.

We heard nothing until Sunday September 4th...

On September 2nd, a church van from Moss Point, Mississippi pulled up in front of Ms. Vera's house!

Moss Point, Mississippi was about three hours away from Waveland, but one of Ms. Vera's brothers was a deacon at the church and had sent them to her home.

This van and several others drove all over Bay St. Louis and the surrounding cities rescuing people.

The van brought Auntie and Ms. Vera to a Moss Point, Mississippi shelter. They were able to shower and sleep in peace.

The next day both the women had someone take them to a motel, which my aunt describes as "like heaven" to them. The first thing she did was take a long, hot, clean bath. How good that bath felt. Then she crawled between the clean sheets of the soft bed and laid her head on the haven of comfort that cradled her. She slept the rest of the day.

The next day was September the 4[th.] My aunt got up early to pack all of her things in her purse. She had arranged for one of the church members to pick her up so that she can go to church that morning. After service, Ms. Sky, one of the members of the church, took my aunt on a one-hour drive to Jackson, Mississippi.

You see, about a month prior to this horrific storm, my aunt had purchased a plane ticket to Oakland, California where her children lived. It had been a few years since she'd seen them and her flight was scheduled to leave on September 4th.

So Auntie pulled out her once "soggy" ID from her once "soggy" purse and boarded her 4:20[pm] flight to Oakland, California. She called my cousin Cassie, her baby-girl to pick her up from the airport.

*Be Still and Know that **I Am God***

*Be Still and Know that **I Am***

*Be Still and **Know***

*Be **Still***

Be

Chapter 6

P.U.S.H.

Pray Until Something Happens!

We arose bright and early the Monday morning of the 5th. We knew the lines would be long everywhere we went, so we needed the earliest start possible. My brother-in-law and I were pumped up. He had an aunt in Humble which was about 45 minutes outside of Houston. This was a much smaller community so we figured we would probably have shorter lines to deal with if we went there and he was right! We walked in and completed our information in a matter minutes. All five family representatives that made the effort were in and out within 45 minutes.

Unfortunately, not everyone saw the favor of God upon us and still continued moaning and complaining. My husband and I tried to ignore it, but it made things hard.

We had to go to the George R. Brown Convention Center where the Red Cross was set up. We needed to register for emergency funds, supplies and medical care for ourselves and our children. The lines at this place were wrapped around the entire convention center twice, but favor was still upon us and this I believed. My husband spoke it as we drove into the parking lot. "Favor, we speak the Favor of God upon us as we take care of our business and we pray that all is done in a timely fashion. Peace rested upon us and moved forward.

Before I could approach the line, I questioned a security guard as to which line was the one I should be in for my particular situation. He pointed toward a loooonnng line. "I have to stand at the end of that?" This line stretched outside the convention center through the parking lot, down the street and underneath a bridge. This was ludicrous! We were on a time schedule and this would take all day and possibly the next. He said wait, let me make sure, come this way.

We walked straight in to the building, past all the lines. He spoke to someone, who spoke to someone else who waved me over to her station. I sat down and she entered all of my information on the spot and handed me a credit card with 1,500 dollars on it! God was showing up and showing out!

I text messaged my husband on his cell who was parking the car. He couldn't believe that I was telling him to walk past all those lines outside and meet me inside at station F. I was now signing up for the medical benefits. We both were seen for general physicals on the spot and received prescriptions for our ailments. We were able to sign up for medical benefits for the children, which would come in the mail.

When we saw the favor God was granting us, in all these things we were doing, we knew God was *moving* in our lives.

All we needed to do was to keep moving forward and keep the negativity out of our mouths and hearts.

We needed to concentrate on noticing what God was doing and being extremely grateful for that, knowing that He hears us and wants to Bless us. None of us on this earth are more worthy than any other. We *all* are dipped in sin. Those of us who implement His principals shall gain the victory over any situation.

About this time, we became desperate for child care for our two babies, my eleven-month-old son and one-year-old granddaughter. I sent my cares up to God. (1 Peter 5:7).

We were riding in the car and passed a child care van. I felt an innate urge to capture the phone number and give them a call. I couldn't find the pen fast enough and it almost got away from me but I was able to get the number saved into my cell phone. I called from my husband's phone (mine still wasn't working). "Hello, Star Kids Day Care", the young lady answered. "Hello, my name is Sandra. My family and I are evacuees of Hurricane Katrina. We're in the process of taking care of a lot of business in order to rebuild our lives and are in need of child care for our 1-year-old and 11-month-old children. How much do you charge?"

I hoped that explaining the fullness of my situation would entitle me to some sort of discount, but it didn't. "$125 per week per child" she said. Whoa! That's $250 per week. And with no job, no home, no food or clothes for four teens, two babies and ourselves, that was way too much for us right now. "If you'd like you can call back and speak to the owner, she should be here in about an hour". Cool, a light at the end of the tunnel.

We moved forward and I was very optimistic about the conversation. I prayed, God please go before me and knead the heart of the owner that she may bless us with a substantial discount, like free.

I don't know how I had the audacity to expect free, but that's what I wanted. One hour later I called back. The same young lady answered the phone. She recognized my voice and asked me to hold. "Hello, this Bula" The woman spoke in a thick African accent.   "Hello Ms. Bula, my name is Sandra and I'm an evacuee of Hurricane Katrina…", I was calm and she listened as I repeated the plight that I had become accustomed to repeating daily, sometimes several times per day.

"Ok my baby", Ms. Bula responded. "You may bring the children and I will charge you $50 per week per child, until you can pay me more; but you go down to The Worksource and apply for child care assistance." "Oh! Thank you, I replied. It wasn't free but $100 instead of $250 was a great discount. Now we had to look at our finances and make it work. She gave me her business address and the information on The Worksource. It was still early in the afternoon, so we went straight to Star Kids Day Care. Ms. Bula turned out to be a true woman of God. She too was a Pastor's wife. Eventually my husband and her husband became close friends, and my husband became a regular speaker at their church.

It was close to 3^{PM} when we made our way to The Worksource. God had been guiding our steps most of the morning and granting favor in every move we made. I could clearly see him moving in my life and I was determined that this would be no different.

My mother taught me through the way she lived that God can do anything, so don't simply accept "no" for the answer, especially when God has put it in your heart otherwise. She also taught us that as Christians we didn't have to take the same route as the rest of the world because we operated with God. She taught me how to be still on the inside and tap in to my Holy Spirit which God promised would be my compass in this earthly realm. (John 14:26)

I got "quiet" enough to hear the Holy Spirit. When I first started understanding and applying this principle to my life, in order to get still on the inside, I would simply stop all that I was doing, close my eyes and say quiet...quiet...quiet...quiet...quiet, until my flesh began to calm and peace would overcome me. At this point I would make my request known unto God and His small, still voice would guide my direction.

I prayed. I need child care for these children, Lord, while we rebuild, please Father God, cover me and guide my steps. Help me connect with your angel, the person you have set in place to make this happen. Then I began to walk through parking lot, toward the door of The Worksource.

As I walked in, I spoke within my spirit. "Holy Spirit, guide me toward the angel that is here to help me". On the inside, I was still quiet. A woman approached me and asked if she could help. I felt jittery on the inside, the quiet peace was interrupted, and I knew that this was not the person to unload the fullness of my needs, so I simply told that her I needed to sign up for child care assistance. She pointed me toward a row of desks at the back of the room.

As I walked, again I prayed. "Father God, guide me toward your chosen vessel". I was quiet as I connected with the Holy Spirit on the inside of me. As I slowly walked I was drawn to a particular gentleman, then I asked "is this your angel Lord"? Within my peace, I could feel the quiet yes. I felt peaceful as I stood still.
I stood facing his desk as he worked with the person who was in front of him. Patiently I waited. "May I help you,"

he said to me as I began to approach him." "Hi", I said and I began my plight. "My name is Mrs. McKnight". I shook his hand. "I am an evacuee of Hurricane Katrina. I am in need of immediate child care assistance for my two babies so that I can focus on the areas that I need to rebuild in my life. I am forced to go to many business offices and it is next to impossible to move efficiently with two one-year-olds. Are you able to help me?"

He spoke. "Ma'am we've had about twelve families in here already today, trying to get assistance, and numerous in the previous days. They're not offering any emergency assistance right now. I can take your information and put you on the waiting list and when the grant money opens up again you will be on the list to receive funding, but honestly that could be several months from now".

"Sir, I need assistance now", I insisted. "Do you have supervisor I can talk to"? "Yes in our corporate office", he replied, "but I've been on the phone with them several times today, as the families have been coming in and *if* they answer the phone, they instruct us to tell them there is no funding and to add them on to the waiting list".

"Please call them again" I asked. He said "ma'am, I can't guarantee I'll get through. The last two times I called, we had to let the phone ring 20 to 30 minutes before anyone answered the line."   "Please call them again" I urged and he dialed the number. An elated look came upon his face when the lady picked up on the second ring. He began to explain who he was and that there was a lady here who was an evacuee of Hurricane Katrina and she wanted....I interrupted with my hand out, "may I speak to her please?" I nodded my head, urging, "may I speak?' "Sure", he said, "uh she wants to speak with you" and he handed me his phone. "Good afternoon", I began, operating in the stillness of my composure. I told the lady the same thing I'd told this gentleman earlier. "Ma'am we're not offering any child care assistance at this time." She said. I'd expected this. My previous sales experience has taught me, you have get through the no's to get to the yes's.

"May I speak to your supervisor please", I asked. "Sure" she said. "Please hold". Another lady answered the line with a slight Spanish accent "This is Maria, How may I help you"? I again repeated my plight. Her response, "hold please". I waited on the phone, and honestly I thought there was another person coming to the line that I would have to repeat everything to. I had repeated these words so many times that I had devised a clear precise description that wouldn't leave much question and would help me to get out all the information I needed them to know, in the fewest words possible. Sometimes I could be a very impatient person, so this helped me with my impatience. The gentleman on the other side of the desk fiddled around with the computer and various items, as the telephone's receiver cord stretched across his desk.

The same lady came back to the phone line. "Ma'am we are going to go ahead and supply you with full funding for both your children for 30 days beginning tomorrow. After that you will be charged based upon your income". Wow! God is good! Our child care was free after all!

My thank you's and smiles caught the attention of the gentleman across the desk as he reached for his pen and pad. "We will need some information from you" she said. I repeated her questions out loud for the benefit of the gentleman on the other side of the desk who eagerly wrote down the details her requests. She then spoke to him about how to handle these matters with future evacuees.

Another Door God Burst Open!   Our child care was free! So was the child care of any evacuee who came there after us! God was showing himself mightily throughout this entire ordeal and we gave Him all the glory, with a mighty "Thank You Lord!"

By the heat & rain

of thundering volcanoes

earth rose & took shape.

The power of His Holy Spirit

absorbed every Atom as He Blew...

activating life.

For us, He created the Earth, the Sun,

the Moon and the Stars,

and us,

He fashioned with His own hands,

& filled with His Holy Spirit.

Made of Earth,

Walk in Dominion here and

over all the land,

For He created us to reign with Him forever.

Chapter 7

Completion

We had lived in my in-law's home for about a month now and it was getting to the point when we needed our own home.

One Sunday we'd visited a church that Bishop Brister was scheduled to preach. After service I ran into someone I'd known from New Orleans. She said there was a broker there a few moments ago who was handing out his business cards and stating that he had homes that he would like to place evacuees in. We wouldn't have to pay anything for a few months and then we can purchase the home or take on his lease-to-own option. I wrote down the information.

My husband and I visited several of the homes the broker had to offer but none of them felt right for our family, for one reason or another.

Even though he was offering them for free for three months we had to pass. I wanted a place I could stabilize our family in and we could build from for the next couple of years. None of these were that place. Finally he convinced us to come into his office and apply for a loan to purchase a new home. I was excited about this option. I had only been temping at my job for one month and my husband owned a landscaping business in New Orleans. It wasn't up and running yet; he was waiting on God for the tools he needed to rebuild his business. The broker assured us that our lack of income wouldn't be a problem and that he could work with our prior tax records and bank statements from before the storm along with our current income from the temp agency.

My sister-in-law on the other hand, had found a house around the corner from hers for us to move into. Red flags and sirens went off in my spirit.

To me, my sister-in-law treated my husband and I as her younger siblings. She fussed, yelled and pushed at us as if we were her children. She was a great help in a lot of ways, but she didn't respect certain boundaries within our lives and I couldn't deal with that. Around the corner was too close to set the boundaries I needed to set.

"I've schedule an appointment with my realtor for this evening at 6^{pm} to look at the house I found for ya'll", my sister-in-law informed us.

I was irritated. My husband was optimistic.

On the way to work that morning one of the ladies I carpooled with told me about this house that had crossed her desk at the housing authority. I don't remember much she said, because I was too focused on the fact that we had a 2:00 appointment with the broker to discuss our loan for the house my sister-in-law found for us. I was not feeling great about it to say the least.

We sat in the broker's office as he went over all of our financial records. He still couldn't make it come together for the loan. He began to move some money around and find areas where he could falsify income statements. He said he would need us to get my brother-in-law to say that my husband is working for him and create receipts. My husband spoke up. "I'm sorry, but I'm a man of God and I can't do any wheeling and dealing to make this happen. If we can't get the loan legit than I guess we can't get it."

The word from last night's Bible Study rang in my spirit. "When God suddenly changes your course, don't question it, go with God".

My cell phone rang. It was Ms. Agnes who I carpooled with to work, calling from her job at the housing authority. "I just wanted to call you and give you the information on that house I told you about this morning." It's a four bedroom, 2½ bath..." as she read the description, my spirit began to leap inside of me. It sounded beautiful. She also said that the owner specifically requested that a family who were Katrina evacuees be placed in the house. FEMA would take care of paying the housing authority for one year."

This was it, I could feel it. There was too much pressure about buying a house right now and I knew God was changing our course to relieve some stress.

I was excited but how would I convince my husband. I hung up the phone, sat up straight and looked directly at the broker. "Last night in Bible Study, I received a word from the Lord. 'When God changes things, don't question it, go with God.' " This was more for my husband's hearing than for theirs. I continued, "right now, I believe that God is changing our course. I just received a call about a house and we need to go check it out". My husband made some comment like "here we go again, chasing rabbits", but I ignored him. I knew what God was saying to me. "We need to go. Is it possible you can Mapquest the directions to this address for us from here?" I felt what New Orleaneans would call "a little cheeky" for asking them to do that, but they did it.

We drove to the house. It was far, but far from what? We had no base home. We made our way to Katy which was about 35 minutes away from my sister-in-law's house.

I loved the serene neighborhood we drove through. This area of town was different from Houston. It was peaceful, clean and beautiful. As we neared the address, we passed a swimming pool and tennis courts at the neighborhood homeowner association. Another block down we pulled in. The house was absolutely beautiful! It was the largest home on the block. And it was amazing. It had everything we believed God for in a home and more. I jumped out of the car.

The owner wasn't able to meet us that evening. We scheduled an appointment to meet her at 9:00 the next morning.

I peered through the large windows in the front of the home, and into the large spacious rooms inside. There was a dining room, with a doorway that led into the kitchen. I could see the large sliding glass door at the back of the kitchen.

From the other window, I could see an office and a doorway that led into a hallway, then into the large living room area. I ran around back, and Oh my God! There was an island in the center of the huge kitchen! I always wanted an island in the kitchen, but I didn't add that to my list.

You see when we were in New Orleans we had learned a scripture principle that stated that we needed to write the vision and make it plain. (Habakkuk 2:2) We had been in the beginning stages of having a home built from the ground up, in New Orleans. This enabled us to write the vision and forced us to design the type of home we wanted.

We wanted a large four bedroom house. We decided that this would be enough space for us and all six children, two people per room, Rodney and I, Sharice and Zya, Samuel and Tank (the boys), and Cache and Courtney (the girls).

My husband wanted a garage that sat toward the back of the house away from the street, because his business required trucks and large equipment that needed space to load and unload.

We wanted a two-car garage and I wanted a two story house with the master bedroom upstairs, so that I can get extra exercise as I went to and from my room each day. We both wanted an office. He for ministry and me for my home-based greeting card company I operated in New Orleans. We both also wanted lots of windows. Our home in New Orleans barely gave us outside light. We had to use in-house lighting day and night. We also wanted our house fully carpeted for the benefit of the babies.

This house had everything we believed God for plus lagniappe (the little extra) blessings from God.

I loved growing up as a child with all the fruit trees we had in the back yard. This house had a lemon, orange, persimmon, pomegranate and banana tree in the back yard. It also had a magnolia tree in the center and a large palm tree that hung over the gazebo. Yes, I said gazebo! And not just any kind either, our gazebo had a brand new hot tub in the center of it. Everything was beautiful.

This is my house! I could feel it through every fiber of my being that this was my house! I couldn't see all of it, but what I could see as I peered in through the windows of the front and back yard, confirmed that this *was* in fact my house!

My husband walked around quietly. I think he was still a little irritated about making him look at another house (chasing rabbits). But I also knew he knew that this was our house!

I was bursting with excitement as we drove back to Houston. We still had to stop at the jewelry store to pick up a gift for Courtney, my step daughter, who's birthday was today, October 6th, and meet up with everyone at the house for cake and ice cream. Oh yeah, and we still had that appointment with my sister-in-law's realtor friend to see the house around the corner from hers.

We pulled up in front the house and the garage door damn near met us at the curb. Beep...wrong answer...we need a garage that sits toward the back, not at the curb. It was all wrong already.

Neither my sister-in-law nor her friend had made it there yet. We sat in the car and waited. The realtor drove up a few minutes later and let us in. We walked into the small dank living room and into the kitchen. The few windows it had brought in very little light and the two of us could barely fit into the tiny kitchen. This two story house was smaller than an apartment was in some areas. The master bedroom was on the other side of the kitchen; I don't even remember what it looked like, all I knew was that it was supposed to be upstairs according to what *we* believed God for.

My sister-in-law came in. "See" she said, "This would be a perfect starter house for ya'll". Starter House, I thought to myself, we're done with "starter" everything. If we were buying a house, it was going to be our home that our grandchildren would come to visit.

I knew this wasn't my house, so I stood at the front doorway while they went upstairs to look at the other two bedrooms. A three bedroom house was not going to work for our family, our vision was four.

"What's wrong with her!" my sister-in-law asked my husband. He'd already told her over the phone earlier about the house we were looking at in Katy. "She wants the house in Katy", he informed her.

"Katy is too far away!" she shouted. "You don't need to move to Katy, and if you do I'm not coming out there to help you!" "Whatever", I thought to myself, but I held my peace and stood in the opening of the front doorway with my back to them. "It's what she wants" my husband told her. "So you are just going let her make all of the decisions and break up our family!" she yelled. "What", I thought. I couldn't believe what I was hearing, this made me turn around, but God knows I kept my peace. My husband spoke up. "Yes, she's my wife and even if it is the wrong decision, we have to do this together." "Good answer", I thought. I didn't like the wrong decision part, but overall good answer, so I turned back toward the outside of the house.

She loomed toward me. "What's so special about this house in Katy?" she yelled. "It's what I want" I said. "Katy is far and you're gonna' have hell in that traffic to and from work, and if you move to Katy, I'm not coming out there to help you out!" "Ok" I said. "I will never forget what you said!" she yelled. "I'll forgive you, but I'll never forget!" I had to think back; what had I said that caused that reply? She then jumped into her SUV and barreled out of there. I thought the vehicle was about to tip over the way it fish tailed around that corner.

And guess what, we still had to go back to the house to celebrate Courtney's 20th birthday and live for another month. Thinking back, I guess I could have handled that episode a little better.

November 5, 2005, on my best friend/cousin Hassann's Birthday, we finally moved into our new home!

Ms. Sharon Jackson, the owner and a sweet woman of God, said she loved this home and wanted to invite a family who would enjoy living here to occupy its space. She also went through great lengths be sure that a family affected by hurricane Katrina took residence. I loved her!

Our new home was absolutely gorgeous! It's a four bedroom, three bathroom house. We have a dining room and an office.   The kitchen is large, complete with dishwasher, garbage disposal, double oven and center-island stove.

The laundry room is on the other side of the kitchen with its own door, closing it off from the rest of the house. We have a large living room with a beautiful brick fireplace. The mantel reached the high ceiling and was almost as wide as the wall in dominated.

Every room had large windows in them, but the living room had three, all facing the beautiful green back yard. The lemon and the orange trees rested against both ends of the windows, and their leaves made a frame when looking out into the yard. This was so beautiful to me. I wanted to accentuate that in my decorating. I bought shear cream curtains for those windows, so we could always have the green of the back yard peering through. It was amazing.

We divided the four bedrooms. Sharice and her daughter Zya would share the larger room. The boys Tank and Sam would share the next largest room, and we put double beds in the third room for Courtney and Cache, and/or houseguests whenever the girls were away in Louisiana. We are a blended family, therefore we have to share our off spring part of the year.

I absolutely loved the master bedroom. It was large with shutters on the windows and two closets (I loved that!). It had a sky window in the bathroom and two sinks. It also had two shower heads in the tub on each end. My husband loved the tub, not only for that reason, but by him being over 6 feet tall; tubs were usually too small for him to bathe in comfortably. This was a huge tub, where even he could lay in.

God was answering our deepest prayers that we'd forgotten we'd prayed and hadn't even added to our vision list. My breath was taken, and I was truly grateful to say the least.

Houston was great to us! One of the organizations we signed up with gave us new mattresses for each person, dressers for each person, six lamps, a coffee table, a small couch and a dinette set seating six.

Our new home even had a room over the garage that was complete with a full bathroom, walk-in closet and three large windows. It even had a window unit supplying air and heat.

We decided that this would be my husband's office space, due to him being a minister and needing a quiet place to retreat and study. Men in general need that, especially with a family as large as ours. It was perfect! The house was complete and perfectly suitable for our family.

I soon found out that Katy school district was one of the best in the country. Wow, we came from the least to the best. God was definitely moving on our behalf. In addition to that there was something called an HOV commuter lane on the freeway that got us from Katy to Houston (directly to my job) with no traffic!

Soon after moving in, God settled me into permanent employment, through the temp agency, at the Houston-Galveston Area Council, ironically, the corporate office of The Worksource. I never did locate the lady, Maria, who God used to help us receive free child care. I wanted to thank her personally. Looking back, I see that God definitely guided my steps to be in this place.

My sister-in-law and I apologized to one another and developed a great relationship.

About three months into our stay at our dream home our landlord stopped receiving the money FEMA had promised. She was put in a position to evict us and I was stressed. I couldn't lose my house! Lord knows I cried out to God.

Then one day she called and asked me if we wanted to buy the house? Again, I cried out to God, and we went back to our broker. Surprisingly enough, the seven months I'd spent as a temp employee was enough to add to our credit and we were approved for the loan. Three months later we were owners of our dream home which was exactly seven months after peering in though its windows. God is truly amazing! We designed the vision and God provided the means to bring it into fruition.

Dear Heavenly Father,

Thank you for resting, ruling and abiding over our lives, for you never lost sight of us.   We know it was you who guided us and kept us safe during this ordeal, and we thank you Father God.

Thank you for never allowing any weapon that comes against to prosper.

Thank you Father for reminding us that we were created in your image to have dominion in this earthly realm and the devil is under our authority. All he can use against us is F.E.A.R. – false evidence appearing real. The Bible teaches us he is as a roaring lion with no teeth, therefore, he has no real power within him and relies on our power to defeat our own selves.

Thank you for removing the blinders and allowing us to see clearly Lord. We stand strong in you Father God. We claim the victory over our lives, and we give you all the Glory, all the Honor and all of the Praise, in Jesus' Holy Name. Amen.

DeLaSandra "Sondra" McKnight, was born on Mardi Gras day in the beautiful city of New Orleans, Louisiana.

Her love for writing poetry evolved from writing in her journals on to owning a spiritual greeting card company called Living Water and her literary journey continues as she leaps on to becoming a powerful novelist.

On August 29, 2005, Hurricane Katrina devastated New Orleans and changed her life and the lives of her family dramatically. Forced to move forward in Houston, Texas, she was determined to persevere in the midst of her trials and gain the victory over this life's circumstances.

She answered her call as an author, by writing her first book, *The Spirit of New Orleans* on September 9, 2009.

Sandra then penned her next book *Step Into Your Divine Destiny and Live Your Life On Purpose.* These and her other works are featured at www.ladymcknight.com.

Made in the USA
Coppell, TX
10 September 2021